THE BUILDINGS OF
ANCIENT EGYPT

Helen and Richard Leacroft

WILLIAM R. SCOTT INC. (PUBLISHER) NEW YORK

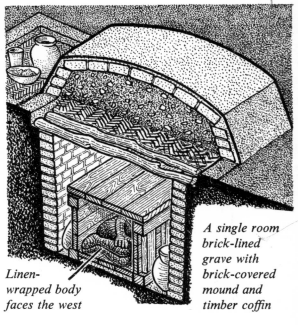

A single room brick-lined grave with brick-covered mound and timber coffin

Linen-wrapped body faces the west

Hidden treasure in fabulous quantities has been discovered and dug up from beneath the warm sands of Egypt. This treasure belonged to people who lived from three to four thousand years before the birth of Christ. However, archaeologists do not spend their lives digging up the past just to find gold, silver and precious stones, but to discover the remains of temples, tombs, homes, furniture, and all the everyday things that help to tell how the ancient peoples lived.

In early times the fertile banks of the River Nile were inhabited by many tribes who probably lived in simple tents or reed huts. These peoples came under the control of powerful rulers who set up two kingdoms of Upper and Lower Egypt; eventually, around 3200 B.C., these two kingdoms were united under one king or pharaoh. From this time a great civilization began to grow up which, over the thousands of years of its existence, left many monuments; some of these can still be seen today, but many more were destroyed or crumbled into the dust which blows across the valley burying even the greatest of the buildings.

The Ancient Egyptian believed in a life after death which he imagined would be a continuation of his life on earth. So when he died he had buried with him all those things that he thought he would need. He built his house and other everyday buildings to last at the most for his own lifetime; but his tombs and temples had to last for ever, and so it is mainly those buildings that have survived for us to explore, and it is to them that we must first turn to learn about these ancient peoples.

In earliest times, when Egyptians died they were wrapped in reed mats and buried quite simply in an oval or rectangular hole in the ground. Buried with them were the pots of food and the weapons that they would need to feed and protect them in their new life. It was considered most important that the body be preserved as a home to which the Soul or *ba* could return from its travels. While the body remained buried, the warm sand and dry climate helped to preserve it, but the simple mound covering the grave could easily be disturbed. To stop this happening, the graves, which had now become rectangular, were lined with timber boards or mud brick. The mound, covered with mud bricks, was usually supported on timber poles. This rectangular mound is called a *mastaba*.

2

*Five-roomed
brick-walled grave*

buried, the mastabas were often robbed. As a result efforts were made to hide the burial chambers, and in later stages of tomb development these were cut out deep below ground-level. Here they were surrounded by the storage rooms, which were arranged like those in a house, even bathrooms and lavatories being sometimes provided for the use of the dead man.

The burial chamber might be at the bottom of a shaft, or be reached by stairs or a sloping passage from the northern end of the mastaba. When the body and goods had been placed in position, the openings were blocked with stones and the passages filled with rubble and sand. Extra protection was often given by lowering great stones down shafts, like the portcullis gates of medieval castles (see bottom of next page). All the shafts and passages were then filled in and the entrances hidden, but although all these precautions were taken it did not seem to occur to the builders that robbers would still know where to look, as most tombs followed a common pattern.

Kings' tombs were always grander than those of ordinary people, and as they had more provisions and goods, a great many storage rooms had to be provided. Some of these were dug around the burial chamber, but more were built inside the mound. This was now made to resemble the home of the owner, the outer brickwork being shaped and painted to look like the posts and reed mats from which these early houses were built. Around the mastaba were small tombs for the servants who accompanied the early kings into their new life.

Since many valuable possessions were now

A ROYAL TOMB AT SAKKARA CIRCA 3200 B.C.

*The mastaba has been cut open
to show the inside*

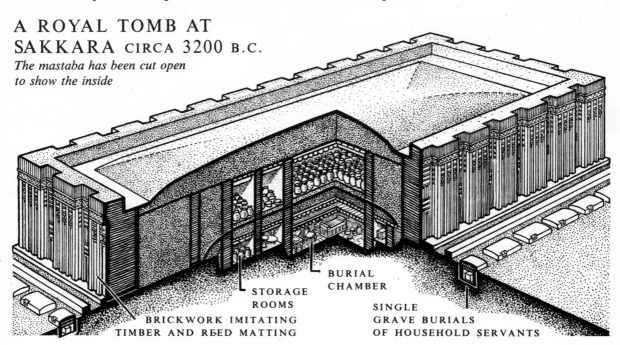

STORAGE
ROOMS

BURIAL
CHAMBER

BRICKWORK IMITATING
TIMBER AND REED MATTING

SINGLE
GRAVE BURIALS
OF HOUSEHOLD SERVANTS

3

FALSE
DOOR

SERDAB
WITH
STATUE

CHAPEL
WITH FALSE
DOOR AND
OFFERINGS
SLAB

*This mastaba and the
rock beneath have been
cut open so that you
can see the inside of
the mastaba and the
burial chamber*

BURIAL SHAFT
BEING FILLED
WITH SAND
AND RUBBLE

BURIAL CHAMBER
WITH SARCOPHAGUS

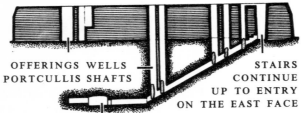

OFFERINGS WELLS
PORTCULLIS SHAFTS

STAIRS
CONTINUE
UP TO ENTRY
ON THE EAST FACE

BURIAL CHAMBER
AND STORAGE ROOMS

NORTH ➤

BRICK MASTABA
of the period of King Zoser, c. 2660 B.C.

After the time of King Zoser the mastabas were faced with stone, which was more permanent than brick. The outer walls were now quite plain, except for two false doorways in the eastern face for the use of the *ba*, and before which offerings could be made.

The offering of provisions to the dead man had always been a feature of Egyptian religion, and in the archaic burials food had been placed on a mat beside the grave. This offering area

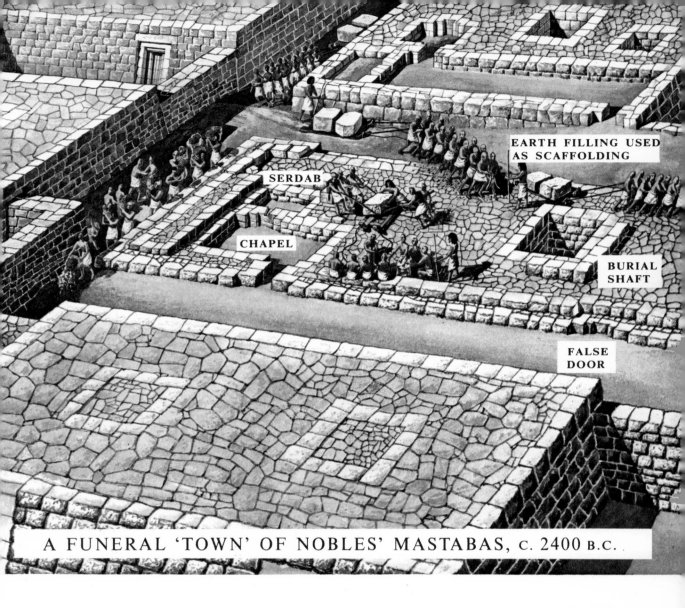

SERDAB

CHAPEL

EARTH FILLING USED
AS SCAFFOLDING

BURIAL
SHAFT

FALSE
DOOR

A FUNERAL 'TOWN' OF NOBLES' MASTABAS, C. 2400 B.C.

was often surrounded by a low brick wall, which later developed into a small chapel. This was usually built before the southernmost door, as this was the door used by the *ba* when it went in and out of the tomb. Later the chapel was moved inside the mastaba and the false door was then built in the chapel's western wall.

To make sure that the dead body was preserved for use by the *ba*, it was now mummified by removing the insides and treating the remainder with preservatives before it was wrapped in linen and laid in a coffin or sarcophagus. As the body might be destroyed, realistic statues were placed in a small secret room – *serdab* – from which the chapel could be seen through narrow slits. These statues could represent the actual body, but in case these too should be damaged, the owner's name was inscribed on them, so that as a last resort the *ba* could return to the Name.

5

Such tombs were expensive to build and only the nobles and important people were buried in this way; the ordinary people continued to use the earlier simple forms of grave. But for the kings even the great mastaba was no longer grand enough, and although the architect Imhotep – 'Chief of all the works of the King of Upper and Lower Egypt' – started to build a simple mastaba for King Zoser, using stone for the first time, he enlarged this several times and eventually covered it with a great mass of masonry built in four steps; even this was not sufficiently imposing, and a much larger stepped 'pyramid' was finally built with six steps, rising to a total height of some two hundred feet.

The burial chamber was at the bottom of a shaft 92 feet deep, off which were a series of gallery rooms lined with timber boards or blue tiles imitating reed matting. These were approached by a sloping passage from the north face of the pyramid, against which were built the *serdab* and offering chapel. This had now become a temple with two open courts and a number of chapels and store rooms, roofed with stone slabs carved to represent the earlier palm-trunk ceilings and painted red, which was the colour used to represent wood.

Both temple and pyramid formed only a small part of this great funeral work, which is thought to have been laid out within its surrounding wall to look like the palaces and courts of the king's residence at the capital, Memphis.

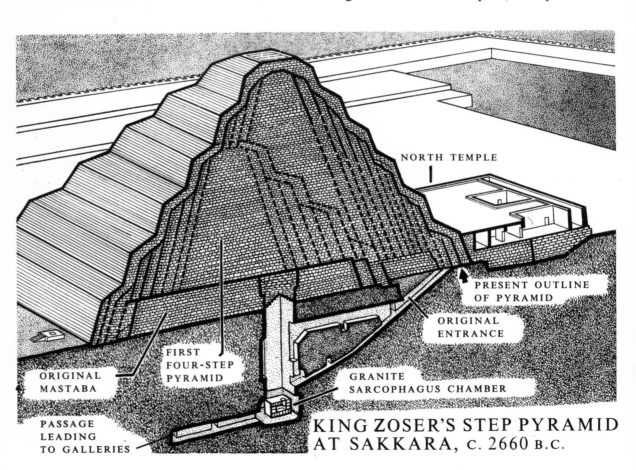

NORTH TEMPLE

PRESENT OUTLINE OF PYRAMID

ORIGINAL ENTRANCE

FIRST FOUR-STEP PYRAMID

ORIGINAL MASTABA

GRANITE SARCOPHAGUS CHAMBER

PASSAGE LEADING TO GALLERIES

KING ZOSER'S STEP PYRAMID AT SAKKARA, C. 2660 B.C.

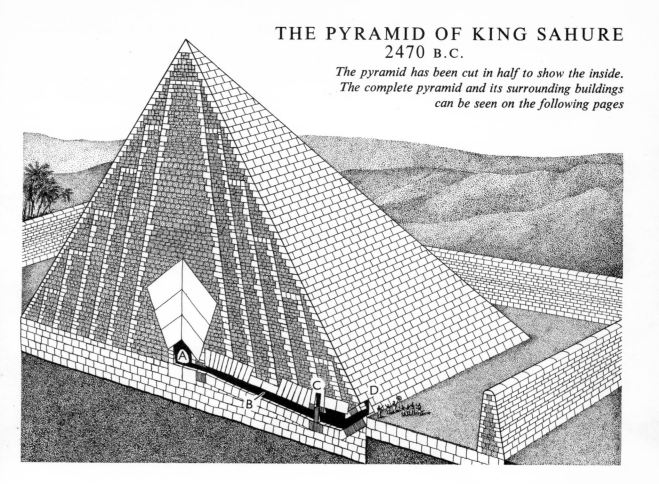

THE PYRAMID OF KING SAHURE
2470 B.C.

*The pyramid has been cut in half to show the inside.
The complete pyramid and its surrounding buildings
can be seen on the following pages*

Some two hundred years after Zoser built his step pyramid, this pyramid was built for King Sahure. Although the outer faces of limestone blocks met at a point at the top following the lines of a true pyramid, inside it was built like Zoser's pyramid with a series of stepped faces carefully smoothed off. You can see how small is the actual burial chamber (A) compared with the solid mass of the pyramid. The only entrance was by a narrow passage (B) from the north face of the pyramid. After the body had been placed in the burial chamber, and everyone had left, the stone (C) was allowed to fall into place completely blocking the passage. The rest of the passage was then filled in with stones and the entrance (D) carefully hidden.

Adjoining the main pyramid was a smaller pyramid containing the queen's tomb. In some cases boats were buried beside the pyramids in which the king could have made his journeys across the sky in company with the Sun God. The gilded stone crowning the pyramid may well have represented the sun as described in a hymn carved in one of the pyramid burial chambers: 'Heaven hath strengthened for thee the rays of the Sun that thou mayest lift thyself to heaven.' All the writings which were carved or painted in the tombs and temples were in picture signs; the Greeks gave them the name *hieroglyph*, which means sacred sign.

7

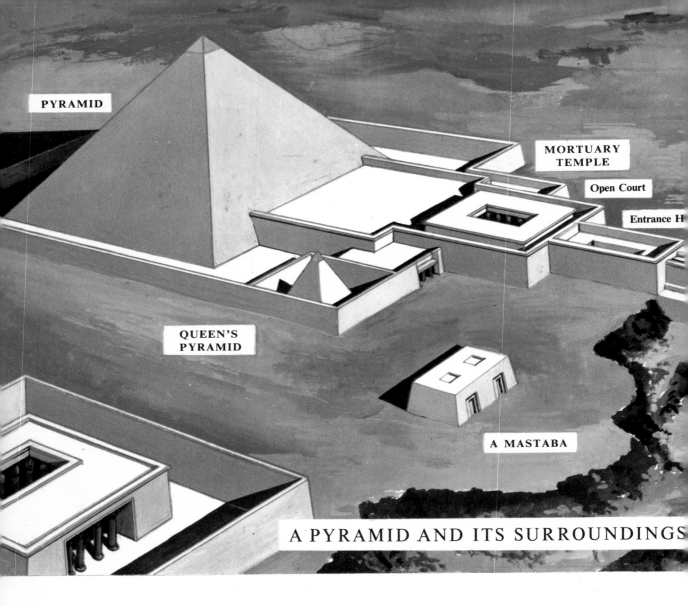

PYRAMID

MORTUARY TEMPLE

Open Court

Entrance H

QUEEN'S PYRAMID

A MASTABA

A PYRAMID AND ITS SURROUNDINGS

The Offering or Mortuary Temple was no longer built against the north face of the pyramid, but was now placed, like the mastaba chapels, on the east face. An entrance hall led into an open-columned court, beyond which was a covered area containing a chapel in which there were five shrines. Directly adjoining the pyramid face was the inner sanctuary. Surrounding these rooms were numerous two-storied store rooms, each pair having its own stair. A staircase led up to the temple roof. ✳Most pyramids were built on the raised plateau of the Western desert. The body of the dead king was brought from his capital in a procession of boats, and disembarked at one of the landing stages of a Valley Temple; this was at the foot of the cliffs, and would have been connected to the capital by a canal. Here the king's body was mummified and purified, after which it was moved to the Mortuary Temple

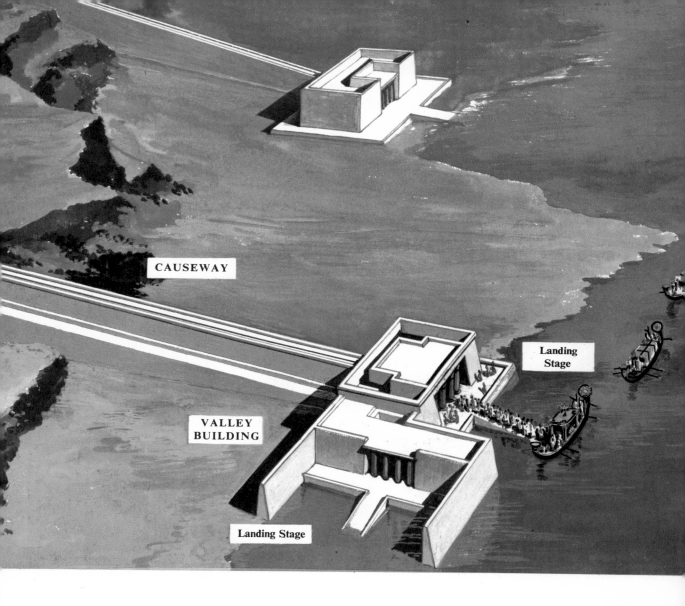

CAUSEWAY

VALLEY
BUILDING

Landing
Stage

Landing Stage

along a walled causeway hidden from the view of the people. This causeway was roofed, with an open slit to let in light, and its walls, like those of the temples, were covered with carvings showing the life and deeds of the king.

✳ We do not know for certain how pyramids were built, but it is most likely that ramps were used, up which the stones could be dragged on sledges to each succeeding level of the pyramid by the multitude of workers employed on the project. These workers would have been drawn from among the *fellahin* or peasants who would have been available for work in large numbers at the time of the annual flooding of the Nile, when they would have been unable to cultivate their fields. According to Herodotus, smaller groups worked in three-monthly shifts for the remainder of the year with a permanent team of skilled craftsmen, who were responsible for preparing and laying the stones.

THE ROCK-CUT TOMB OF
SETI I, 1320–1301 B.C.

BURIAL CHAMBER:
here the King's mummy—his preserved body—was placed in the great stone sarcophagus, marked 'C'. This is now in the Soane Museum, London, while his mummy is in the Cairo Museum. Today the tomb is lit by electricity, and you can examine the paintings on the walls in reasonable comfort

BLIND ROOM: *it is possible that this room was originally intended to be the burial chamber. The tomb was then extended and this room was abandoned, and used to help in deceiving any intending robbers. The doorway at 'A' and the floor at 'B' were both filled in, and the openings hidden for the same purpose*

STORE ROOMS
for the funeral furniture, etc.

For many centuries the pharaohs built tombs of the pyramid form; the greatest and best known being those at Giza near Cairo, where there is a group of three pyramids, the largest of which was built by Cheops, and a surrounding 'city' of mastabas (see pages 4–5). Later pyramids were smaller, an example may be seen in the tomb of Mentuhotep on page 15. In the early sixteenth century B.C., when the capital was moved to Thebes, the kings tried to hide their tombs, and they were cut out of the solid rock in the Valley of the Kings. The narrow entrances to this valley were guarded, and because there was no room in the valley, and as an extra precaution, the mortuary temples were built some distance away, so that the site of the tomb was no longer marked above ground. But in spite of all these precautions most of the tombs were robbed. Above can be seen a drawing of one of the

10

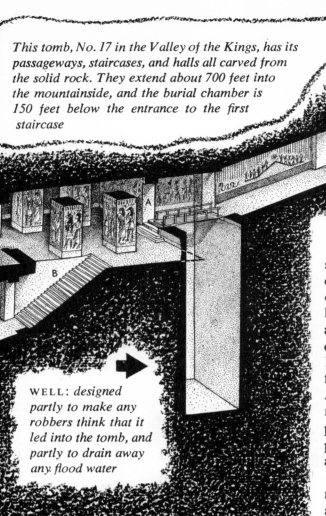

This tomb, No. 17 in the Valley of the Kings, has its passageways, staircases, and halls all carved from the solid rock. They extend about 700 feet into the mountainside, and the burial chamber is 150 feet below the entrance to the first staircase

MAIN ENTRANCE TO THE TOMB *from the Valley of the Kings*

WELL: *designed partly to make any robbers think that it led into the tomb, and partly to drain away any flood water*

some of whom were Eater of Blood, Breaker of Bones, Eye of Flame, White Tooth, and Leg of Fire. In the presence of the god Osiris the king's heart was weighed in the balance against a feather, and only if it proved lighter was he declared innocent of sin and admitted to the Hereafter. If, by some mischance, he was found to be a sinner he was devoured by Amemit, the Devourer, Eater of Souls, a female monster with the head of a crocodile, the fore-part of a lion and the hindquarters of a hippopotamus, or he was turned into a black pig and driven to the place of punishment.

At a very early date the practice of burying members of the king's household had been abandoned. Instead the idea of representing the owner of the tomb by a statue was developed, and in the tombs of the nobles their families, servants, and possessions were pictured on the walls, together with scenes of their work and pleasures such as hunting, fishing, and feasting. Later on models of houses and servants were also placed in the tomb, and it is largely from these pictures and models that we can discover the life of these ancient peoples. Illustrated on the first page of this book is the inside of a noble's mortuary chapel. This shows some of the wall paintings, and on the far wall his funeral ceremony may be seen.

finest rock-cut tombs; it extends a long way into the mountainside, and has many halls and rooms for storing the household goods and furniture.

The walls of the passages and rooms of the tomb were covered with paintings and texts which would ensure the safe passage of the dead king through the Underworld, and help him to answer the questions of the forty-two animal and human-headed gods, the names of

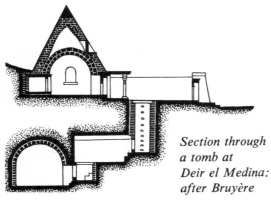

*Section through
a tomb at
Deir el Medina:
after Bruyère*

Here is the funeral service of a noble of the mid-fourteenth century B.C. Although the pharaohs had given up the pyramid as a tomb form, it was still used by the nobles, who combined it with the house form of the period to make a chapel, with its open portico and walled courtyard. The mummified body has been ferried across the Nile from the city of Thebes, and dragged by a pair of oxen to the tomb on a boat-shaped sledge decorated with lotus flowers, and

followed by the servants carrying all those things which are to be buried with him. In the far corner of the courtyard another sledge carries a chest which holds the jars containing the dead man's internal organs.

In front of the chapel the ceremony of Opening the Mouth is being performed, when the priests, one of whom represents Anubis the jackal-headed god of Death, and the eldest son restore the vital functions to the mummy, by opening the eyes and mouth with special instruments and the foreleg of a bull. After this the mouth is touched with sacred tablets and the mummy is embraced by the son. The women of the family wail, and the noble's wife throws dust on her head to show her sorrow.

After the ceremony all the goods are stored away, and the mummy is lowered down the open shaft to the burial chamber; then the shaft is filled and the entrance hidden.

13

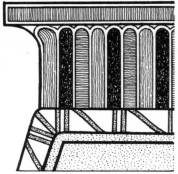

Early reed and mud type hut, showing strengthened corners and decorative cornice

Kheker type ornamental cornice

Hieroglyph of the Anubis shrine

Detail of cornice and roll as used to crown walls, pylons, and doors

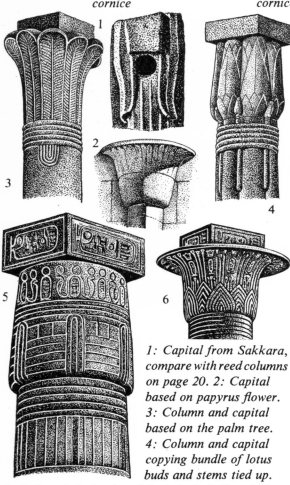

1: Capital from Sakkara, compare with reed columns on page 20. 2: Capital based on papyrus flower. 3: Column and capital based on the palm tree. 4: Column and capital copying bundle of lotus buds and stems tied up. 5: Bud capital, developed from 4. 6: Bell capital developed from 2; see also pages 21, 22, and 23.

The Ancient Egyptians wanted their tombs and temples to last for ever, so they built them of stone. We have already seen the way in which they copied earlier ways of building when they used a new material, and they did the same thing when they used stone, most likely because the earlier forms had come to have a religious meaning.

Early buildings were made from reeds or palm fronds, matted together and strengthened with reeds tied in bundles and fastened at the corners and across the tops of the walls. The heads of the vertical reeds, left free above the walls, provided a crowning decoration which was the basis for the *kheker* ornament painted on so many tomb walls, including those in our first picture. Reeds tied in bundles could also be used as columns–see page 20–and these and the walls when plastered with mud became quite strong, but they did not have a long life.

These tied reed bundles were later imitated on the stone walls and pylons, and the shape of the coved cornice which crowns all doors and walls probably came from the untied reeds curving above the early walls. Even the stone columns were carved to resemble the bundles of papyrus stems, with their flowers forming a decorative head or capital; or the palm tree with its fronds or the lotus buds tied round the posts.

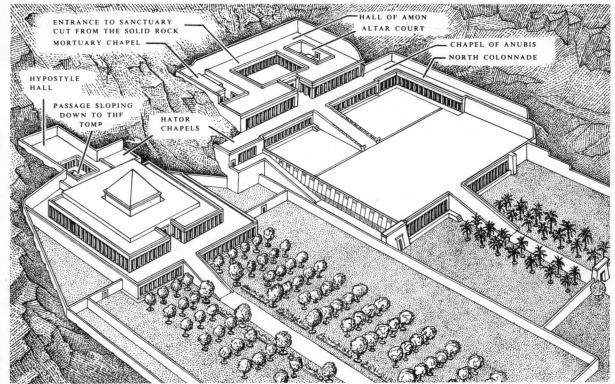

ENTRANCE TO SANCTUARY
CUT FROM THE SOLID ROCK
MORTUARY CHAPEL

HALL OF AMON
ALTAR COURT

CHAPEL OF ANUBIS
NORTH COLONNADE

HYPOSTYLE
HALL

PASSAGE SLOPING
DOWN TO THE
TOMB

HATOR
CHAPELS

*Two mortuary temples at Deir el Bahri, Thebes.   Left: Pyramid temple of King Mentuhotep, c. 2010 B.C.
Right: Temple of Queen Hatshepsut, 1503–1482 B.C.*

The two mortuary temples above show stages in the change from the earlier pyramids situated above the burial chamber, to the temple separated from the tomb. In the temple on the left the burial chamber was approached from the courtyard behind the pyramid, but in the building on the right the burial was in the Valley of the Kings on the other side of the cliffs in which the inner sanctuaries of both temples were cut.

As well as mortuary temples there were other temples built as homes for the gods. These god-temples had developed from the house of the chieftain who was generally considered to be divine, as were also the later pharaohs, many of whom, like Ramesses II at Abu Simbel, built temples to the gods and to their own greater glory.

Great temple of Ramesses II, Abu Simbel, c. 1270 B.C.

15

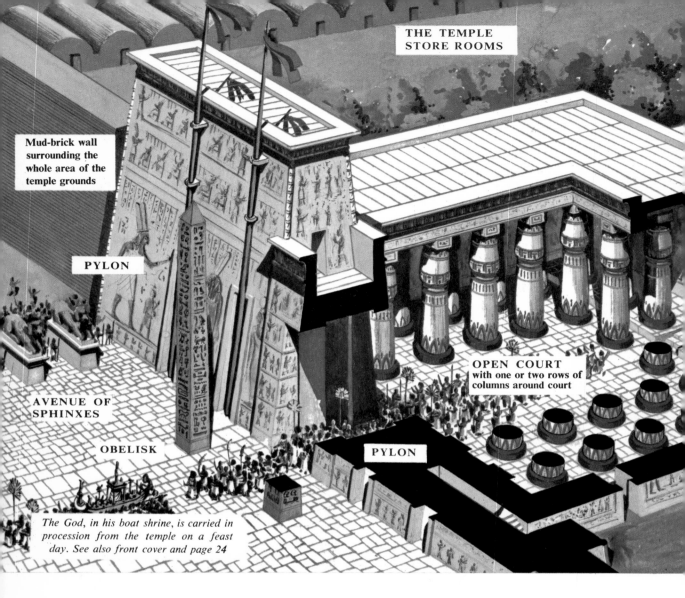

THE TEMPLE
STORE ROOMS

Mud-brick wall
surrounding the
whole area of the
temple grounds

PYLON

OPEN COURT
with one or two rows of
columns around court

AVENUE OF
SPHINXES

OBELISK

PYLON

*The God, in his boat shrine, is carried in
procession from the temple on a feast
day. See also front cover and page 24*

The typical parts of a later god-temple are well
illustrated in this small building based on the
temple of Khons at Karnak. Here can be seen
the approach through the avenue of sphinxes to
the doorway in the great pylon, adorned with
flagpoles and painted carvings showing the
pharaoh making offerings to the gods. Both the
pylon and the surrounding walls were built
with a batter on the outer face: that is the wall
was reduced in thickness the higher it rose, a
system of building which probably derived from
the earlier mud-brick structures.

The open courtyard had colonnades on one,
two, or three sides. No uninitiated person could
pass beyond this through the central door leading to the *hypostyle*–many-columned–hall,
beyond which an inner hall led to the sanctuary
where the god dwelt. Surrounding the sanctuary
were store rooms for the possessions of the god,
and for use at special ceremonies. Further

16

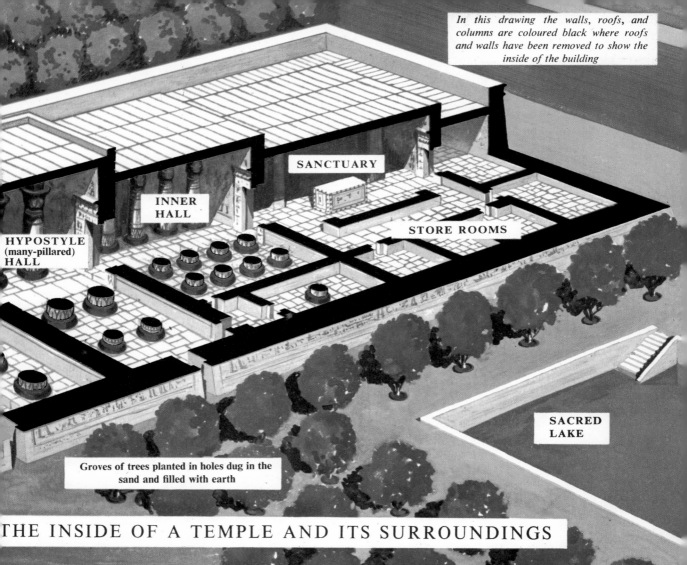

SANCTUARY

INNER HALL

STORE ROOMS

HYPOSTYLE (many-pillared) HALL

SACRED LAKE

Groves of trees planted in holes dug in the sand and filled with earth

THE INSIDE OF A TEMPLE AND ITS SURROUNDINGS

priestly store rooms were built round the temple, and these were often made of mud brick with tunnel-like roofs.

As Egyptian life centred about the life-giving waters of the Nile, boats formed an important part of existence, even the shrine of the god being boat-shaped. The sacred lake of the temple was the source of water for purification, and here certain religious ceremonies were performed by the priests.

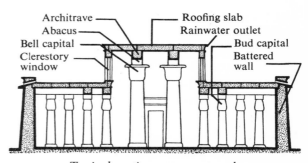

Architrave
Abacus
Bell capital
Clerestory window
Roofing slab
Rainwater outlet
Bud capital
Battered wall

Typical section across a temple

17

In the darkness of a limestone quarry the stones are cut with chisels and split by wedges

When the Egyptians built a large hall they used rows of columns to support the roof. On top of each column was a square *abacus* (as on previous page) and these supported the ends of the stone *architraves* which spanned from one column to the next, and in turn supported the thick stone roofing slabs.

Limestone, sandstone, and granite were all used for building, depending on which was nearest and most convenient. When the capital was at Memphis, limestone from the Tura quarries was used. Granite was used in the temple of the Sphinx at Giza, but this is a very hard stone which is difficult to work, and it had to be brought all the way from Aswan, so it was seldom used for building. When the capital moved to Thebes, sandstone from the quarries at Silsila was used. This was stronger than the limestone, which could not be used to span

A team of oxen drag a stone on a sledge, from the Tura quarries

more than eight or nine feet. The Egyptians liked to make their temples as large and as grand as possible, and the use of sandstone enabled them to span distances as great as 30 feet.

At Silsila the stone was quarried near the surface but where the stone lay deeper, cavelike quarries were cut out of the cliff face. As may be seen in the drawing on page 18, the stone was cut in an orderly pattern of roughly rectangular blocks. At the top of the stone face some three feet of rock was cut to waste so that the quarryman could cut down the back and sides of the stones with a copper chisel which he struck with a wooden mallet. The blocks were separated from the rock beneath by driv-

ing in wooden wedges over which water was poured to make them swell.

Hard granite was not easy to cut with a chisel, and so wedges were used to split the stone, or it was pounded out by using balls or mauls made of a hard stone called dolerite. The top rock was broken up by alternately heating and cooling the stone. Each man had a two-foot wide section of separating trench to cut away, the overseer marking off the depth of the stone on the rock face.

Surface quarrying of Granite. Fire and water break up the top stone, then dolerite balls and mauls are used as well as timber wedges

Three scenes from the tomb of Rekhmire, Vizier of Upper Egypt, c. 1471–1448 B.C. showing sculptors (top and centre) and masons (below) at work

Disused buildings were often robbed of their stones to save the trouble of quarrying; this is one reason why many buildings have not survived to modern times. But wherever the stones came from they were dragged along on wooden sledges drawn by men or oxen. If they had to be moved a long distance, they were ferried along Egypt's main highway, the River Nile. In the drawing a convoy of barges is carrying stones from the quarries.

The rough stones were shaped and placed on rockers so that they could easily be moved to make a tight fit against each other. They were then dragged to their positions in the building on a wooden sledge up a ramp made of brick, earth, and timber balks, which was raised and extended as the building went up. The remains of some ramps may still be seen today. Water was poured in front of the sledge to help it run, and a man beat time with clappers.

20

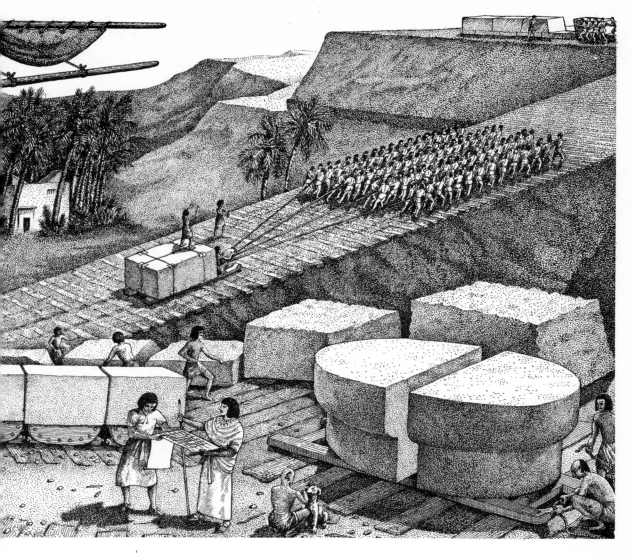

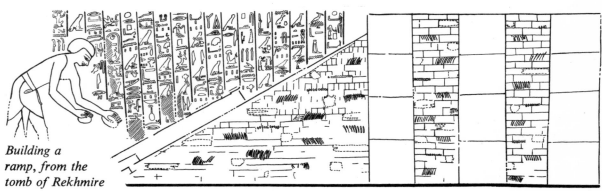

Building a ramp, from the tomb of Rekhmire

A painter, standing on scaffolding, decorates a new pylon. Wall painting from the tomb of Rekhmire

The Ancient Egyptians had to move all their building materials by manpower because they had no cranes or mechanical equipment. At first this was not serious because they used small stones, but when they increased the size of their buildings they used huge blocks weighing many tons. When the stone had been dragged up the ramp it was levered into position, mortar being used to help it slide easily into place.

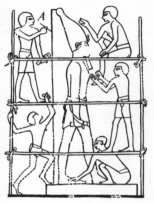

A painter (A) and sculptors put the finishing touches to granite statues of the pharaoh. From the tomb of Rekhmire

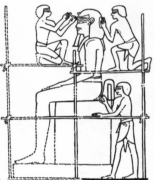

When a temple was begun they placed in position all the stones of the lowest course, or layer, of the walls and columns. The spaces between were then filled in with earth to make a new 'ground-level'. Over this the stones for the second course could be dragged and placed in position; more earth being added. As the building gained height the stones were dragged up the ramps built against the outer walls, and eventually, when the roof had been put on, the building was entirely full of earth and surrounded by brick and earth platforms.

The earth was gradually removed, and as the walls and columns came once again into view, they were smoothed to their final shape, and the carving and painting was added. In the picture the 'floor' is still some sixty feet above ground-level, and the painters and sculptors are working on the great capitals of the hypostyle hall.

24

Left: The king makes offerings before the portable boat shrine of the god in the Sanctuary. From the chapel of Osiris in the temple of Sethos I at Abydos. Right: A boat shrine in procession for the Opet Festival. From the temple of Amon at Luxor

Daily worship in the temple was a religious dramatization of everyday life. The god was awakened each morning with hymns, he was washed, perfumed, dressed, and given a meal. Then he either remained in the darkness of the sanctuary or, preceded by the high priest in his leopard skin, was carried in his boat shrine by a procession of priests to the outer court. Here he received offerings and petitions, and gave judgements. At special festivals he was carried in his boat shrine out of the temple – as page 16. Each day there was a short service at noon, and a longer one took place at sunset when the god retired to bed.

Modern Bedouin with their tents and camels

We have found out how tombs and temples were built. Now we must see what the houses of the Egyptians were like. The first wandering tribes probably set up shelters of reeds to protect themselves from the wind and sun, and later lived in tents, similar to those of the modern Bedouin but made of skins or hides. When the people started to cultivate the land they needed more permanent homes. A clay model found in a tomb shows a house which appears to be a development from the tent. In our drawing the roof is supported by mud-covered reed pillars; there is also the suggestion of the open loggia of later tombs and houses, and the walled courtyard in front of the house where the cooking and many household chores appear to have been carried out.

A second type of house was made of reeds daubed with mud, such as may still be seen in some Sudanese villages. An early carving of a hut shows a similar shape, but it has a curved roof which was made by bending reeds into a dome shape.

It would seem from early pictures of house shrines that a form of light-framed house was used by the ruling classes. These houses were probably built from small lengths of wood skil-

Sudanese huts

Left: Reconstruction of a reed hut, based on an ivory carving from an early tomb at Abydos.
Below: Reconstruction of a tent shelter, based on a clay model from a tomb at Rifeh

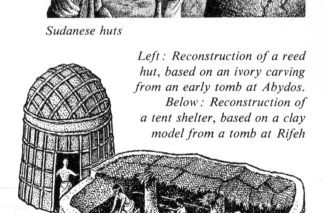

26

fully jointed together; reed matting covered the curved roof, which may well have been built of bent reeds. The door was set to one end of the house to ensure privacy for the occupants. The spaces between the timber framing were probably filled with reed matting, which could be let down during the heat of the day or when a sandstorm was blowing, and rolled up in the evening to let the cool breezes blow through the house.

At the bottom of the page is an illustration of a stone sarcophagus which has been carved to represent an early frame and reed matting house, such as was copied in brick in the early mastaba seen on page 3. Wood suitable for building has never been plentiful in Egypt, the local trees being palm, sycamore, and acacia. The palm, because of its fibrous nature, cannot be sawn into planks, and its only uses were for posts and ceiling beams; only short lengths of wood could be cut from the other trees. All other wood had to be imported, as for example, cedar from Lebanon: this made it expensive, so such timbers were reserved for special use, and some other material had to be found for the main structure.

Reconstruction of an early timber shrine hut, based in part on the Anubis shrine, below

Reconstruction of a mud house, based on a model found in a Predynastic tomb at el Amrah

Shrine of Anubis, from the royal seal of King Zer, c. 3200 B.C.

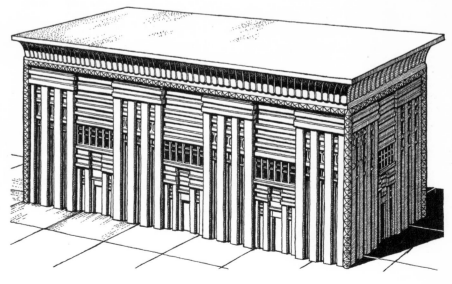

Stone sarcophagus of King Menkaure, c. 2500 B.C. after Perrot-Chipiez

Making bricks for the storehouses of the temple of Amon, Karnak, fro

28

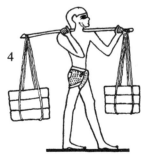

4

of Rekhmire

The annual floods left mud on the fields which dried hard in the sun, and this was made into mud bricks. An early mud hut can be seen on page 27, while above, workers are making bricks and building some nobles' houses.

On the left are some tomb paintings of brickmakers at work. Two men are drawing water from a pool surrounded by trees (1), next a man is mixing mud (2), and other men are carrying mud to the brickmaker, who is using a wooden mould and laying the bricks in the sun to dry (3). Finally another worker (4) carries the finished bricks in a simple yoke to the bricklayer.

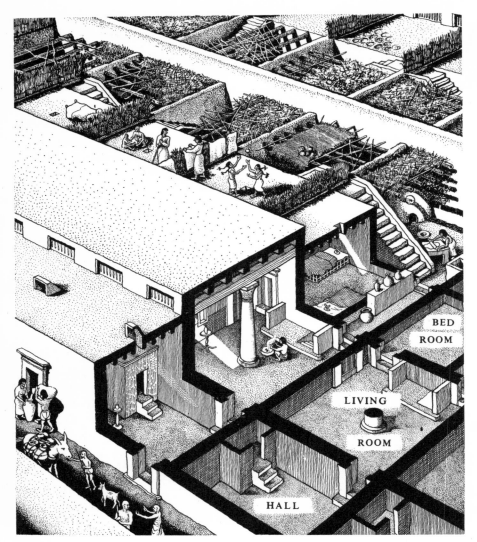

A reconstruction of workers' terrace houses, based in part on the houses in the village of Deir el Medina: after Bruyère. Some of the houses have been cut open so that one can see inside

BED ROOM

LIVING

ROOM

HALL

On any large building operation the workers lived in special villages, which were walled in a manner suggesting that many workers may have been compelled to work; but this does not necessarily mean that they were slaves, although captured slaves were sometimes used. In these villages the houses were built very close together, but they show the basic arrangement also found in the homes of the nobles.

A main central room had minor rooms grouped round it to keep it warm in winter and cool in summer. The living room was carried up higher than the other two rooms so that windows could be built in the upper walls; this clerestory lighting was also used in the temples where the central aisle of the hypostyle hall was carried up higher than the side aisles – as page 17. Because the sun is very bright few windows were needed; even the small hole shown in the bedroom roof let in sufficient light. Windows

Wall painting of a house with ventilators on the roof. From the tomb of Neb-Amun. After N. de G. Davies

were usually slits in a piece of stone or clay set into the wall.

Water was stored in carefully guarded cisterns placed outside the main gates, and it was fetched from here and poured into storage jars which were kept at the entrances to the houses. The front door leads into the hall, in one corner of which is the family shrine. In the roof is a combined light hole and ventilator to catch the wind. Similar ventilators are shown in the painting from the tomb of Neb-Amun at Thebes, and also in the reconstructions of this house which can be seen on pages 21 and 33.

In the living-room a householder is warming himself at a charcoal fire, and behind him is a raised step or *divan*, from which a flight of steps leads to a store room. Opening off the living-room is a bedroom with two beds. On these are the shaped head-rests which were used instead of pillows. A passage leads to an open court used as the kitchen, with an oven in the corner; a light covering of matting shields the housewife from the sun. Steps lead up to the flat roofs made of mud on reeds and palm trunks. Here the children can play and the family sleep on warm nights.

Wherever it was possible the Egyptian liked to have a garden next to his house, with a pool to cool the air, and trees and a loggia to give shade from the hot sun. As most towns were built on land unsuitable for agriculture, trees were planted in holes filled with Nile mud, as can be seen in the drawing below.

The shady tree-planted garden, pool, and loggia of a nobleman's house. After a model found in the tomb of Meket-re

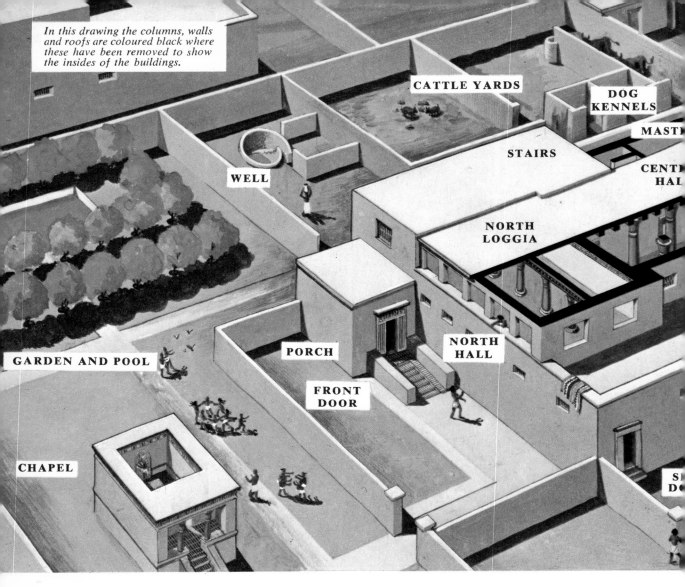

In this drawing the columns, walls and roofs are coloured black where these have been removed to show the insides of the buildings.

CATTLE YARDS

DOG KENNELS

MAST[

STAIRS

CENT[
HA[

WELL

NORTH
LOGGIA

NORTH
HALL

PORCH

GARDEN AND POOL

FRONT
DOOR

CHAPEL

S[
D[

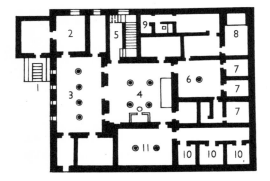

Where there was plenty of room for development as in the new city at el Amarna, a nobleman's house was laid out on a generous scale. This large house stands in its own grounds with a private chapel, servants' quarters, stables, cattle yards, and a large garden with a pool surrounded by trees.

It is entered from the north by a flight of steps (1), which for all their number ascend no more than a foot or two; a flight of steps con-

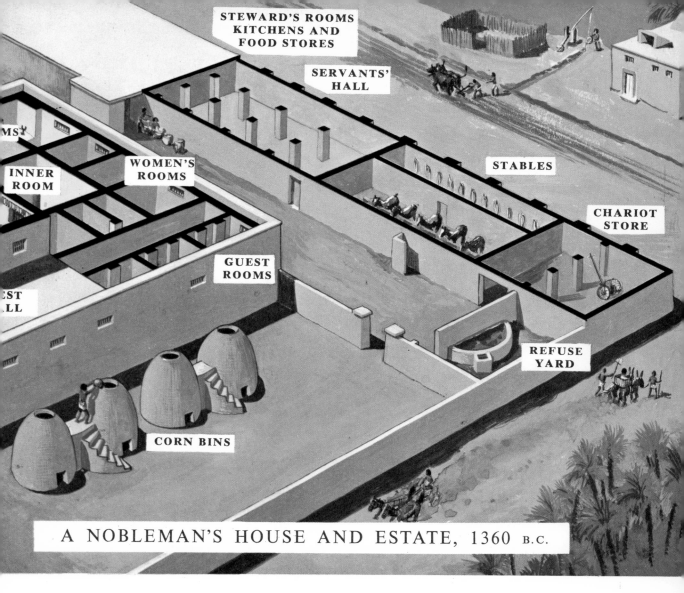

STEWARD'S ROOMS KITCHENS AND FOOD STORES

SERVANTS' HALL

STABLES

CHARIOT STORE

...MS

INNER ROOM

WOMEN'S ROOMS

...ST ...LL

GUEST ROOMS

REFUSE YARD

CORN BINS

A NOBLEMAN'S HOUSE AND ESTATE, 1360 B.C.

ferred social prestige on the owner. A vestibule (2) leads into the North Hall (3) (pages 36–7) which is also approached by a side door for use by the servants. Three doors lead into the Central Hall (4) which, with its four columns, had clerestory lighting above the surrounding roofs. Stairs (5) lead up to the roof and a loggia over the North Hall, which was open to the cool winds. An Inner Room (6) gives access to the women's rooms (7) and those of the master,

which included a bedroom (8) and a lavatory and bathroom (9). The master's bed is on a raised step, beneath which is an opening leading down to a cellar where the valuables can be stored. Separated from the remainder of the house is a suite of rooms for guests (10) entered off a West Hall (11).

The corn bins in the foreground of the picture can be seen to retain the shape of the earlier domed houses.

In those Egyptian towns where space was limited, houses were built with several storeys to take up less ground space. These town houses may well have looked like the one shown at the top of this page. Reed screens placed on the top of the walls made it possible for the family to enjoy the cool evening air without being overlooked from adjoining houses, and open loggias provided some shade so that the roof could also be used during the heat of the day.

The tomb painting below shows what the inside of the house may have looked like. At the ground-level servants are spinning, weaving, and preparing food, while on the floor above they wait upon their master who is seated in the main room. Other servants carry stores up the stairs to the roof and upper rooms, while the master is again seen being fanned and entertained on the upper floor. Corn bins are set on the left-hand roof with two ovens on the right.

*Reconstruction of a
town house, based
on an ancient model*

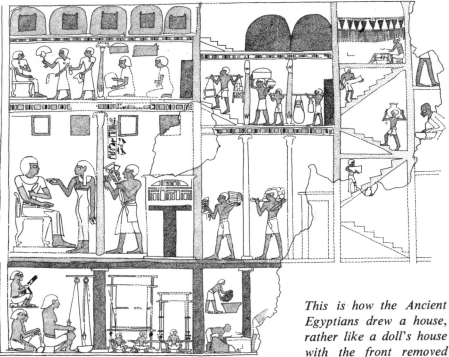

*Drawing based on a
wall painting from the
tomb of Thut-Nufer:
after N. de G. Davies*

*This is how the Ancient
Egyptians drew a house,
rather like a doll's house
with the front removed*

34

Models of household life from various tombs. 1: Servant carrying food. 2: Bakers at work. 3: A drover and bullock. 4: Girl grinding corn. 5: Woman brewing beer

Royal palaces were very like the nobles' houses except that they were larger. They too were built mainly of mud brick. The drawing, bottom right, is an Ancient Egyptian's picture of the Great Palace at el Amarna. Although this does not suggest the wide extent of the buildings that have been excavated on this site, it does present, in a simple way, the main elements of a palace. Today we draw plans and elevations of a building separately, but the Egyptian artist combined them in one drawing.

The palace is entered by one of the gateways (1) in the wall surrounding the courtyard (2). In the centre of the main building is a portico (3) shielding the Window of Appearances (4) where the pharaoh could make his public appearances and reward his followers. On either side doors lead between columns (5) into the great audience hall (6), here seen prepared for a feast, while a servant sweeps the floor between the two rows of columns.

The artist who carved this picture had probably never been beyond the audience hall into the private apartments of the palace. In the palace which opened off the first court of the temple of Medinet Habu at Thebes, a throne room adjoined the audience hall. In this picture the artist shows a passage (7) leading into the king's quarters and his bedroom (8). In the real palace these quarters were much more spacious and included a suite for the queen, and rooms for the ladies of the harem grouped round a private court with flower-beds and running water. Further rooms (9) open off the great hall, here suggesting store rooms; in addition to these, lavish provision was made for court officials, servants, and animals.

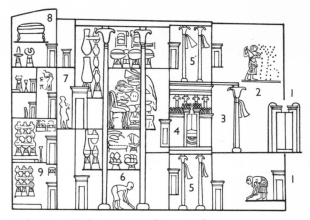

Side view of the Great Palace at el Amarna, from a relief in the tomb of Merya c. 1360 B.C. After N. de G. Davies

Here is the North Hall of the house on pages 32–3, with the Central Hall beyond. The master and his wife are seated on the left; over his shaven head he wears his ceremonial wig, usually made of real hair. His son's head is also shaven save for one lock of hair; he looks at a clay model of a house which his father holds. The wife, wearing a fine linen dress, holds one of the lotus blossoms which decorate the room, while another hangs from her headband so that she can constantly smell its sweet perfume.

The children quarrel and play with their toys or the family cat, while servants bring fruit and make music for the dancing girls, seen also in the tomb paintings – right. Reed mats cover the floor, and special reed stands support wine and water jars, the former decorated with vine leaves. The Egyptians liked symmetry, so here doors were balanced by niches, and window grills merged into the decorative frieze.

Little girls squabbling, from tomb of Menna

Musicians, from an unknown Theban tomb

37

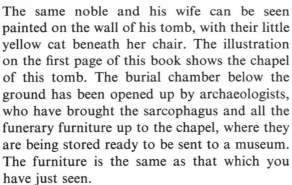

A pottery hippopotamus
in the Cairo Museum

The same noble and his wife can be seen painted on the wall of his tomb, with their little yellow cat beneath her chair. The illustration on the first page of this book shows the chapel of this tomb. The burial chamber below the ground has been opened up by archaeologists, who have brought the sarcophagus and all the funerary furniture up to the chapel, where they are being stored ready to be sent to a museum. The furniture is the same as that which you have just seen.

The paintings, models, and furniture found in the tomb, have been added to the remains of the houses which the archaeologists have excavated, to make a complete picture of one aspect of domestic life at one moment in time in the three thousand years of the Ancient Egyptian civilization.

Because it is largely from their tombs that we have been able to learn something about the Ancient Egyptians, we have had to spend much time describing their burial customs. But you should not think from this that they were a morbid people thinking only of death; it was because life meant so much to them that they liked to think of it continuing into the Hereafter. You have only to look at many of their wall paintings to realize that they could be a cheerful people with a great love of life and a good sense of humour. Look at the picture of the two little girls pulling each other's hair on page 37, and the animals, birds, and reptiles on the map opposite, all of which have been copied from tomb paintings.

Through their buildings it has been possible to catch only a glimpse of the way the Ancient Egyptians lived. There are many more exciting things you may now be tempted to discover about them, which will help you to understand the wonders of the ancient civilization of Egypt.

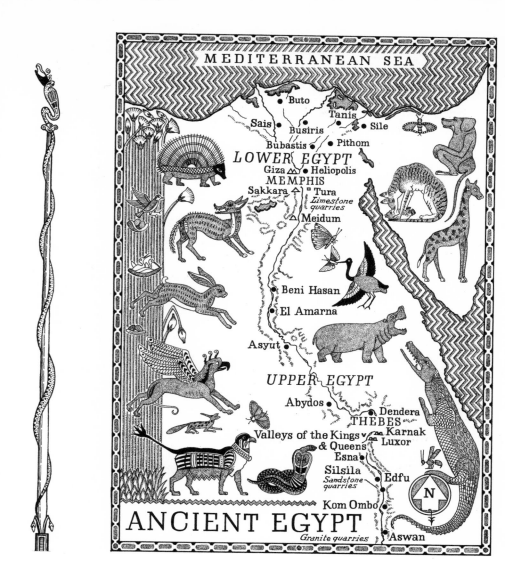

ANCIENT EGYPT

ACKNOWLEDGEMENTS

Sincere thanks are due to Professor H. W. Fairman –without whose patient introduction to Egypt this book would not have been possible – and to Mr I. E. S. Edwards, for their help and criticism in the preparation of the original Puffin Picture Book edition, and to the former for his additional help and advice in the preparation of this revised and enlarged edition.

Thanks are also due to the Egypt Exploration Society for permission to base the drawings on pages 28–9, 32–3, 36–7, on material from their publications, *The City of Akhenaton*, parts 1 and 2, and *The Journal of Egyptian Archaeology*, Vol. 19: to the Metropolitan Museum of Art, New York, for material from the tombs of Rekhmire, Neb-Amun, Merya, Thut-Nufer, and Meket-re: the Harvard University Press for the mastaba, page 4, from Reisner's *Development of the Egyptian Tomb*: the Trustees of the British Museum for the musicians, page 37, and the Leicester Museum for the bakers, page 35.

INDEX

This edition first published in the United States of America in 1963 by William R. Scott, Inc., Publisher, New York
Printed in Great Britain by Jarrold & Sons Ltd, Norwich